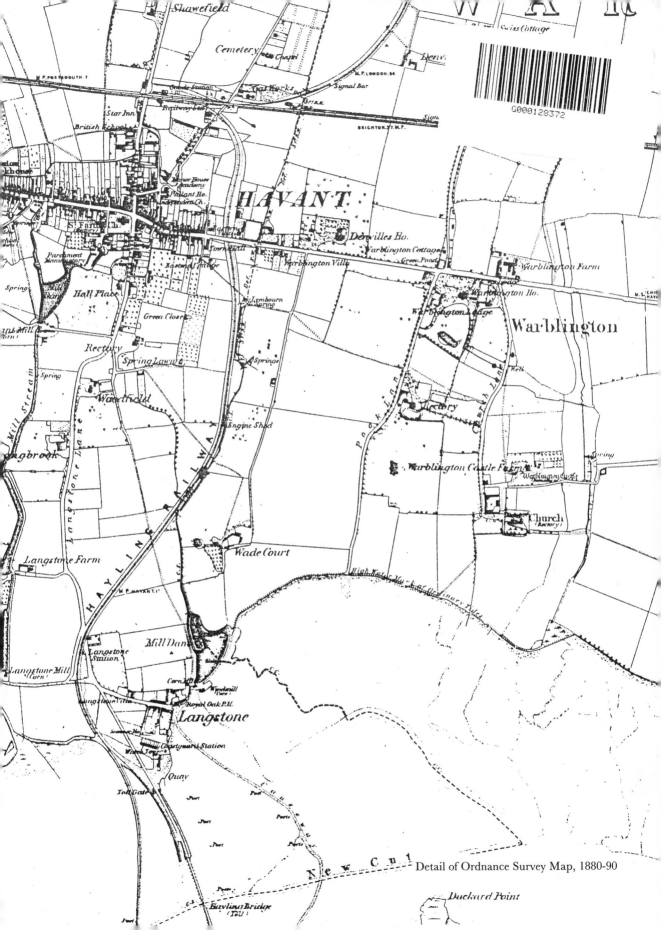

Detail of Ordnance Survey Map, 1880-90

Bygone

HAVANT

A comic postcard of the 1920s.

Bygone
HAVANT

Ralph Cousins
and
Peter Rogers

Phillimore

1993

Published by
PHILLIMORE & CO. LTD.
Shopwyke Manor Barn, Chichester, Sussex

ISBN 0 85033 882 4

Printed and bound in Great Britain by
BIDDLES LTD.
Guildford, Surrey

List of Illustrations

Frontispiece: Comic postcard, 1920s

Acknowledgements

The successful completion of this, the latest addition to an already considerable treatise on Havant, can be attributed to numerous kind friends and colleagues, organisations and institutions who have assisted in making available for reproduction many of the photographs contained within these pages and for permitting access to personal and printed notes from which much of the text has been compiled. We wish to place on record our sincere thanks and appreciation to those who have allowed us to reproduce material which is wholly owned by or under copyright to them: Havant Borough Council, Hampshire County Libraries Service, Hampshire County Museums Service, Curator and staff of Havant Museum, *The News* – Portsmouth, Mr. Alf Harris, Mrs. Evelyn Hedley, Mrs. Betty Marshall, Mr. Reg New, Mr. George Parsons, Mrs. M. Stevens, Mr. Freddie Vine and Mr. Douglas White. Recognised also are the skills, patience and dedication of Audrey Rogers who unravelled the intricacies of handwritten text to produce via the word-processor, a lucid and legible manuscript. As with any acknowledged sources, it is always possible that reference to a particular item or individual has been omitted; our apologies are extended for any such imprudence should it have occurred.

Introduction

In A.D.935 the present town of Havant was recorded with the name 'Hamafunta' which can be translated as 'Hama's spring' and almost certainly refers to the Homewell spring which lies to the south west of St Faith's churchyard.

The presence of this spring near to the crossing point of two ancient tracks, one following the coast and the other coming down from the Downs to the shore, was the main reason for the establishment of a settlement. The convenient proximity of the harbours and forest also meant ample supplies for fishing, hunting and wood.

Archaeological finds indicate that Havant has probably been inhabited for several thousand years. The remains of ancient dwellings have been found near to the Lavant stream to the north of Bartons Road as well as Neolithic instruments at Warblington and Langstone, and Mesolithic flints in East Street. At Crookhorn, just beyond Havant's Saxon boundary, there are the remains of a Neolithic long barrow which was used as a Bronze Age, Iron Age and Saxon burial ground.

In 1832 Roman foundations were discovered at St Faith's church during renovation work and in 1926 the remains of a Roman villa were discovered in Langstone Avenue. The Roman road from Chichester to Wickham followed the present line of East and West Streets and it is thought that another Roman road from Rowlands Castle to Hayling Island crossed it near to the present crossroads, possibly where East Street bends near to the *Bear Hotel*.

Havant is recorded in the Domesday Survey as follows:

> The monks hold Havunte from the Bishopric of Winchester, they always held it. Before 1066 it paid tax for 10 hides; now for 7 hides. Land for 4 ploughs. 14 villagers with 6 ploughs. 2 mills at 15 shillings; 3 salterns at 15 pence; woodland for 10 pigs. The value is and was 8 pounds.

A hide was an area of land between 60 and 120 acres which was considered to be adequate to support one freeman and his family. Land for a plough was a piece of land capable of being cultivated and salterns were sea water pools where salt was produced by evaporation.

Local industries based on agriculture and water developed over the years. The land was suitable for growing corn and grazing, and the supply of fresh water was abundant. Rain falling on the Downs to the north was absorbed by the chalk and channelled underground to emerge from over twenty springs which had a combined average output of 100 million litres of water each day. The Lavant stream, whose source was also in the Downs, added to this supply.

Corn was ground into flour or meal by the many local mills which were built and rebuilt. The remains of the most recent ones are still visible. The Town Mill, dating from 1460, stood to the west of what is now the junction of the A27 and Park Road South and was driven by water coming from the Lavant stream, the Homewell spring and a spring which today is beneath the multi-storey car park. The water was held in a large millpond and released by a sluice gate to drive the water wheel. A separate sluice gate enabled nearby fields to be irrigated. The mill was operational until 1934, and was demolished in 1958 to make way for the by-pass. When an office block was built on the site of the millpond, a symbolic wooden wheel was erected in the old mill race.

West Mill, also called Langstone Mill or South Mill, at the end of Mill Lane was driven by the water which had first driven the Town Mill. It was erected in 1823 in place of a fulling mill which had burnt down in the 1750s, and was pulled down in 1936. Fulling mills were first built in the 12th century for treating cloth which had been home-spun. It was soaked in various solutions and then beaten by heavy wooden mallets, which were powered by the waterwheel, in order to compact the fibres and threads.

Brockhampton Mill stood on what is now the Solent Way just south of the junction of Harts Farm Way and Southmoor Road. It was powered by water from the Brockhampton springs and was demolished before 1900.

The only evidence there is of windmills is the one which stands on the foreshore at Langstone which worked until the mid-1800s. Alongside this mill was a watermill driven by the Lymbourne stream, fed by the spring at the bottom end of Lymbourne Road. The water was held in the millpond which has recently been restored.

The mills by the sea all had quays which could accommodate barges for transporting their products to other parts of the country. During the 19th century, milling became modernised with the establishment of a steam-driven mill in Park Road South.

The pastureland around Havant and on the Downs was ideal for sheep farming which in turn supported a number of other industries. Wool was made into cloth and a thriving trade was established. However, during the 16th century, Parliament introduced a new standard size to which cloth had to be manufactured and as this could not be complied with locally the industry went into decline. The sheep also provided essential food, and their skins were used for the manufacture of parchment and leather.

Havant parchment was held in very high regard on account of its whiteness compared with all other parchment which tended to be yellow. It was made from the inner layer of the sheep's skin which was processed over several weeks before being finished. Throughout manufacture large quantities of spring water were used and it was the unique properties of this water which were responsible for the parchment's whiteness.

Although parchment had been made in Havant for hundreds of years there is no evidence to show that it was produced on any large scale until the 1850s. The last parchment yard, Stallard's in Homewell, closed in 1936.

The outer layer of the sheeps' skins, together with the skins of other animals, went to various tanneries in the town for making into leather. This was another industry requiring a large volume of water. It flourished by supplying boot-, shoe-, clothes- and harness-making trades. The making of leather and high quality gloves continued into the 1960s, much of the latter work being carried out in employees' homes.

Brewing was another thriving local industry also reliant on the abundant supply of virtually pure water. In 1855 there were four breweries and nine malt houses in the town and in addition a number of Beer Houses brewed their own supply. The barley for the malt as well as the hops were grown locally. The last brewery was Biden's which was situated in West Street next to the *Prince of Wales*. When it closed in the 1920s it was converted into a laundry, later becoming the Home Service Laundry, making exploitative use of the brewery's old well. Another laundry, the steam-driven Hygeia in Waterloo Road, also had its own well.

Watercress grew prolifically in the spring-fed streams and provided a very successful business for the Marshall family for about a century until 1960.

In 1200 the Bishop of Winchester obtained a charter from King John granting the town of 'Haveunte' a market every week on the condition that it did not interfere with any neighbouring market. In 1451 Henry VI confirmed this charter and granted an additional charter giving the town of 'Havont' an annual two-day fair on 6 October, the feast of St Faith. This fair was held in the Fair-field which lay to the east of the present Fairfield Road. Also included in this charter was permission for an extra weekly market which was held on Saturdays for the sale of corn. A second annual fair was held on 11 June, the feast of St Barnabas, which took place in the streets and around the walls of St Faith's church. No record exists of any charter being granted for this fair but it has been suggested that a Saxon temple may have stood on the site of St Faith's church before it was rebuilt in about the 12th century, and that this temple had been dedicated to St Barnabas when converted to a Christian church in the 7th century.

When the calendar was altered in 1752 and eleven days, from the third to the thirteenth of September inclusive, were omitted, it was enacted that all markets and fairs were to be held eleven days later. Havant's fairs were held on 22 June and 17 October until they were abolished in 1871.

Sometime after the charter of Henry VI was granted, a market house was built in South Street alongside the church wall. It is recorded as being in a dilapidated state in 1645 and eventually collapsed in 1710. It was rebuilt on the same site and consisted of an open arched passage, an enclosure with standing room for 50, stalls and the usual requirements for a market. There was an adjoining cage which served as a local lock up and the top floor of the building was used as a school and court house for the Lord of the Manor to conduct his business. However, as it was difficult for waggons to pass between the market house and the buildings opposite, it was rebuilt near to the same place but the problem was still unsolved and it was pulled down for good in 1828. Further down South Street there were fish and meat stalls. A Tuesday cattle market was established in the meadow at the rear of the *Star Hotel* in North Street. Around 1900 it moved across the road to Dog Kennel Farm where the North Street Arcade now stands. The loss of many small farms in the area and changes in the method of trading animals eventually affected the viability of the market, so, 756 years after King John's charter, it came to an end in January 1956.

Havant's parish church is dedicated to St Faith, a young girl of Aquitaine in France, who was martyred *c*.A.D.290 during the Diocletian persecution. Whilst unrecorded in the Domesday Survey, there are other references to the church about this time. The early Gothic style is retained despite being rebuilt and restored several times.

The churchyard had always been Havant's principal burial ground and by 1850 it was estimated to hold the remains of over 20,000 souls. Its level had risen to well above that of the surrounding streets and as it became impossible to make new burials without disturbing the remains of others, a new cemetery was established on land in New Lane which had been given by Sir George Staunton. One acre was allocated for the church and a quarter of an acre for dissenters. The cemetery was expanded in 1896.

By 1800 there were several shops and a church house in front of the church in West Street; most of these were demolished at some time but one building remained at the corner of Homewell by the churchyard until the 1920s. The church house was founded for the use of the poor and became a meeting place for social events. Spits, crocks and other utensils for cooking were provided by the parish free of charge and could be obtained from here. The building was later converted into an almshouse, the last occupants being two aged paupers by the names of Bishop and Carpenter.

Examination of the records of the Court Leet, the manorial court which dealt with criminal offences, gives some idea of lawlessness in the 17th and 18th centuries. Havant possessed the usual equipment for the punishment of offenders; the ducking stool, stocks, pillory, whipping post and the lock up. Anyone sentenced to be confined in one of these appliances would become the target of abuse and missiles from their fellow townspeople.

Some of the cases recorded are worth mentioning. Richard Townsend who drew blood with a dagger during a fight with Robert Norrys, fined 3s. 4d. Robert Woods and Nicholas Godfrey for playing cards in the house of Arthur Woolgar, fined 12d. each. Robert Dudman for being habitually drunk, fined 3s. 4d. Joseph Barkett for allowing his wife to wash children's clothes in the Homewell spring, let off but he would be fined 40s. (two pounds) if she did it again. Eleonora Baron, a common scold, was sentenced to the ducking stool. The Rural Police Act was passed in 1839 from which the modern police system evolved. A police station and courthouse were built in 1858 next to the workhouse which stood at the east corner of West Street and Union Road. Prior to this time the petty sessions were held in the upper room of *The Black Dog*.

One of the most important people to have lived in the area was Margaret Pole, Countess of Salisbury, who resided from 1521 until 1543 at Warblington Castle. A relative of Henry VIII, she is reputed to have entertained him there on two occasions. However, Henry later suspected her of helping her son, Cardinal Reginald Pole, in his support for the Pope during his religious battles with the king. Margaret was interrogated at Warblington before being taken to the Tower of London where she was tried and found guilty of treason and executed in 1543.

The castle was completed around 1520 and a survey carried out in 1632 described it as a very fair place, well moated and built with bricks and stone. It was about 200 ft. square and contained a great hall, kitchen, armoury, parlour, chapel and many other rooms necessary to such a prominent family. There was a fair green court within and outside, gardens, meadows, orchards, barns, stables, outhouses and a fishpond. The whole impressive building was dominated by a gatehouse with four towers which housed a portcullis and drawbridge. Sadly, all that remains is the gateway and one of the towers. The castle was later occupied by the Cotton family who supported Charles I. In 1644 a party of Cromwell's men severely damaged the castle and its destruction was completed by local builders and stone robbers. This is evidenced by the fact that material from the castle has been found in many buildings in the area.

Another event which took place at this time was a clash by St Faith's church on Christmas Day 1643. A group of King's men led by the local rector Francis Ringstead put to flight some Parliamentarians led by Colonel Norton of Southwick House. During the Civil War, lands owned by the church were confiscated and the Manor of Havant was sold on 21 February 1647 to William Woolgar for £1,162 5s. 4d. When Charles II was restored to the throne the Manor was returned to the Bishop of Winchester who granted a lease to William.

William's Manor house, which had been built with material from Warblington Castle, was replaced in 1795 by another which was demolished in the 1930s to make way for the building of Manor Close. The lease of the Manor changed hands several times until it was obtained in 1820 by Sir George Thomas Staunton when he bought Leigh Park house and the estate. Sir George was a young man who had returned to England from China having worked for 20 years with the East India Company and was anxious to buy a country estate in order to improve his status. In 1827 he bought the freehold of the manor from the Bishop of Winchester for £2,075 1s. 9d. During his time at Leigh Park he carried out extensive tree and shrub planting, extended the lake and built many bridges, monuments and follies. Next to the house he built a Gothic-style library, which still stands, and large glasshouses that have now been re-erected.

In 1828 he arranged for the Havant to Horndean road, which passed within 30 yards of the house, to be moved further to the east. Also, irritated by having to wait at the Bedhampton and Stockheath level crossings after the railway had been opened in 1847, he had the first part of New Road built linking Bedhampton Road to Stockheath Lane.

Sir George died in 1859 and William Stone bought the house and estate in 1861. In 1863 he replaced the house with a mansion in the north gardens overlooking the lake. During his brief time in Havant he donated the land in New Lane which is laid out as allotments 'to be let for the relief of poverty among the labouring classes of Havant'. He also opened the grounds for fêtes, shows and weekend picnics and permission was given to use the lake for fishing and ice-skating.

These privileges were continued by Sir Frederick Fitzwygram after he bought the estate in 1864 in particular he used the grounds for rallies to woo the electorate during his campaign for election as the Member of Parliament for South Hampshire. The *Hampshire County Times* reported that 'on 28th June he held a Conservative fête the scale of which was never before equalled in the south of England'. He died in 1904 and the estate passed through members of his family until in 1946 it was purchased by Portsmouth City Council who built one of the largest municipal housing estates in Europe on it. Although William Stone's mansion was demolished in 1959 the gardens and ornamental farm were spared and are now, with the addition of other land, being restored and developed into the Sir George Staunton Country Park.

For those who followed the established faith, religious worship posed no problem, although there was a time when a fine was imposed for not attending church. Other religions, in particular the Roman Catholics, found life more difficult. It may, however, have been the presence nearby of a number of prominent Catholic families which influenced the fact that Havant was the centre of Catholic worship for a large area. Also, being situated close to the sea, it was easy to make a rapid escape to the Continent if necessary. Before 1700, Catholics were visited by travelling priests but at about this time a mission was established in Langstone, reputedly in the roof space of a number of cottages. In about 1750 the mission moved to some other cottages in Brockhampton and in 1752 it moved again into a purpose-built building nearby whose outside appearance disguised its chapel within. Stables were provided for worshippers' horses as some had to travel great distances, there being no chapels in Portsmouth or Chichester at this time. However, their situation was relieved by the passing of the Catholic Relief Bill in 1791 but the present church of St Joseph was not established until 1875.

The origin of the church of St Thomas à Becket is not clear but parts of the present building are of Saxon origin. The yew tree alongside is estimated to be over 1,000 years old and it has been suggested that it was planted, along with other yews, on a pagan worship site, and remained after the site was taken over for the building of a Christian church. The church's isolated position is likely to have been the reason for the construction of the flint huts at opposite corners of the churchyard. It is believed that they date from around 1800 and were used by gravewatchers who kept a look out for bodysnatchers. On the south side of the church there is a fine sundial, dated 1781, and carved below in the left hand window jamb is what is believed to be part of a Mass clock. These clocks were used to indicate if it was time for Mass by inserting a rod in a central hole and seeing if its shadow coincided with one of the predetermined lines.

The chapel of St Nicholas in Langstone High Street was built in the 1860s and is still in use. In 1874 an 'Iron church' was built in Brockhampton Lane on the corner of Selbourne Road, so called because it was iron framed and clad with corrugated iron sheets. It was used for services and social events until it was demolished in the 1970s.

The Primitive Methodists built a chapel in 1878 at the end of West Street near to the Bedhampton railway crossing. This had a following of many well known local people and continued in use until the 1950s when a new church was built in Park Lane, Bedhampton. The old building still stands although in a very dilapidated condition. There are records of protestant dissenters being active in Havant during the 17th century and in 1728 they established a church in The Pallant. This church became known as the Congregational church and remained in use until the new church in North Street was opened in 1891. The name was changed to the United Reformed church when the merger with the Presbyterian church took place in 1972.

In the 1880s the Wesleyans decided to build the chapel in West Street opposite *The Black Dog*. In 1932 they combined with the Primitive Methodists and the United Methodists to form the present day Methodist church. Although not very well supported, the chapel continued in use until the 1950s, and today the building is used as commercial premises.

On 25 October 1784 an earthquake was felt in Havant between 3 and 4 a.m. It was reported that it lasted for some two or three minutes and after a short interval it was repeated for another two or three minutes. There then followed a gale which lasted for several hours. A similar experience was repeated on 30 November 1811 at 2.45 a.m. when a violent shock was felt causing considerable alarm amongst the many awoken from their sleep. It is not known if either event caused any damage or casualties.

In about 1760 a serious fire took hold in the town and most of the present day shopping area of West Street and parts of North and East Streets were destroyed. At this time there was no organised arrangement for fire fighting and ladders, buckets, poles with hooks and possibly hand-held pumps were all that was available. It is believed that these were kept at the Market House. There is a reference to the Sun Insurance Company contributing towards the cost of a fire engine in 1788, but usually these engines would only be used if the premises concerned were insured with that company, such insurance being indicated by the company's fire mark, in plaque-form. Eventually the parish obtained hand-operated, horse- or hand-drawn, fire engines and in 1871 the Havant Volunteer Fire Brigade was formed.

Before the fire, the paved roads through the town were very narrow making, it difficult for waggons to pass, and outside the town the roads were described as being 'ruinous and deep'. Rebuilding the houses further apart and the establishment of the Portsmouth to Chichester Turnpike Trust marked the start of improved conditions. A tollgate was installed near to the present location of the Bedhampton level crossing and a charge was levied on all road-users, the profits being used to keep the road in good repair. The Turnpike Trust was in operation until 1867. Better roads greatly improved stagecoach travel and in 1823 departures were advertised from Havant to Brighton, Portsmouth, Southampton and London. The *Bear Hotel*, East Street and the *Dolphin Hotel*, which stood at the present West Street entrance to the Meridian Centre, were important coaching inns. Road traffic started to decline when the London, Brighton and South Coast Railway Company opened its route from Brighton to Portsmouth on 15 March 1847. This improved coastway communications but travellers to London had to go via Brighton or Eastleigh. The more direct route from London terminated at Godalming, and as no railway company was interested in extending the line to Havant, Thomas Brassey, a private contractor, decided to build it as a speculative venture. The first sod was turned at Buriton on 8 August 1853 and the single-track line was completed in 1858.

The London and South Western Railway Company reluctantly took the line over to keep out its rivals, but in order to run a through service to Portsmouth it had to obtain running rights over the L.B.S.C.R. track between Havant and Portcreek. Thinking that these rights had been obtained, it announced that it would run a through goods train on 28 December 1858. However, the L.B.S.C.R. disagreed so they removed a part of the points at the down junction and put an engine across the up junction. The L.S.W.R. train arrived at 7 a.m. with a large number of plate-layers on board. These men moved the L.B.S.C.R. engine into a siding so that their train could go down the up line to the station and over a crossover back on to the down line to Portsmouth. However the L.B.S.C.R. platelayers realised what was happening, removed part of the crossover thus preventing the L.S.W.R. train from moving forward but leaving it blocking both lines. It remained here for several hours before reversing back to Godalming. During the course of this confrontation two railway officials from opposing sides got into an argument and one had his shirt torn. This subsequently became a court case with the one accusing the other of assault. This was the only incidence of violence recorded and it bears no relation to later embellishments of the events of this day, calling it 'The Battle of Havant' with hundreds of men fighting each other resulting in many injuries!

The L.S.W.R. did, however, start a service from London but passengers had to alight at a temporary platform which was erected in Denvilles. They were then taken to Cosham by horse-drawn omnibus, for a fare of 6d., where they caught another L.S.W.R. train into Portsmouth; this was possible as the company had running rights over the line between Portcreek and Portsmouth. The dispute was soon resolved and a through service started on Monday 24 January 1859, but the line between Godalming and Havant remained single track until 1878. The line to Hayling Island was opened as far as Langston (the railway always used the old name without the 'e') on 19 January 1865 but was not extended to South Hayling until 17 July 1867. In 1871 the line was leased to the L.B.S.C.R. who, in 1890, introduced their Stroudley Terrier A1X class engines which hauled trains until the last public service ran on Saturday 2 November 1963. The very last train was a special which ran the next day. Between 1885 and 1888 a paddle steamer called 'Carrier' took goods waggons from a specially constructed berth at Langston to the Isle of Wight.

The original Havant railway station was rebuilt about 1889 and the present 'Odeon'-style station was built in 1938 following the electrification of the lines in 1937. This time the station was moved to the west, blocking off the top end of North Street and its level crossing. This necessitated the building of a new bridge and roads to take the north-south traffic around the town centre.

The Health of Towns Act was passed in 1848 and on the 30 July 1851 a petition was presented to the General Board of Health requesting that an inspection be carried out to see if the provisions of the Act should be applied to Havant. A subsequent enquiry, which took place in the *Bear Hotel* on 2 October 1851, recommended that a Havant Local Board of Health (Town Council) should be elected. This was arranged and the first meeting was held at *The Black Dog* on 3 June 1852, where the state of water, drainage and sewerage systems was discussed. At this time water was obtained from springs and wells but in 1857 the Portsmouth Water Company was established and a mains supply was brought to Havant in 1870. A start was made on the drainage and sewerage systems but took many years to complete.

Authorisation was given for the Havant Gas Company to be formed which built a gas works in New Lane (renamed Gas House Road), north-east of the level crossing. The works was in operation by 1855 supplying commercial and private customers as well as 33 streetlamps. In 1926 the Portsea Island Gas Company took over the Havant company and production ceased but some of their buildings remain. Electricity reached Havant from Portsmouth in 1923 and gradually replaced gas for streetlighting although one lamp from the 1930s can be seen outside the Havant Museum, now lit by North Sea gas.

Havant's poorhouse was built some time before 1800 and stood to the east of the junction of West Street and Union Road. In 1814 it was occupied by 8 men, 12 women, 12 boys and 12 girls. The men and women were kept busy doing housework or tending the allotment garden whilst the boys and girls were employed picking oakum; this was hemp or jute fibre which when tarred was used for caulking the seams in wooden ships. Surprisingly, a person was employed to teach the children to read.

Under the provisions of the Poor Law Amendment Act of 1834 the parish of Havant became the centre of the Havant Union which comprised the parishes of Havant, Bedhampton, Warblington, Farlington, North Hayling and South Hayling. Each parish sent representatives, called Guardians, to sit on the Board of Guardians which was responsible for the running of the Union Workhouse, as it was now called, and the distribution of relief in the parishes. At this time the old poorhouse was extended so that it could accommodate up to 200 inmates although it was never thought to have held more than 150. The Poor Law Institution, as it was finally called, closed in 1936. The main building was demolished in 1947 but its mortuary remains as part of the Horticultural Society Trading Store in Park Way.

There was no formal requirement for state education until the Education Act of 1870 which required Local Boards to be set up to provide places for all children between the ages of five and thirteen. Before this time, education in Havant had been provided by a number of private schools, both large and small, in addition to a few church and Sunday schools.

In 1829 a British school was established in Market Lane, now Market Parade, followed later by an Anglican National school in Brockhampton Lane. A small school was also built at Warblington on the corner of Pook Lane and Emsworth Road. In the 1870s the Church of England built a school in School Road, off Brockhampton Lane, and this continued in use until the 1950s. The building is now used as commercial premises. When the Roman Catholic Church was built in West Street in 1875, a school for about 40 children was provided at the rear of the Presbytery. The Havant Board school in Fairfield Road, now Fairfield First school, was not built until 1895. In 1902 a further Education Act passed the control of schools to the Hampshire County Council and Board schools became elementary schools for children between the ages of 5 and 14, and were referred to as Council schools.

The public postal service was started in 1635 and Havant is recorded as having a postmaster in 1768. The post office itself has been in various locations in the town; in 1827 it was in a shop in West Street and in 1846 it moved to another shop at No.4 East Street. It established its own premises in 1892 at No.6 West Street and stayed there until 1936 when it moved to its present location in East Street.

In the early 1900s there were two telephone companies operating in Havant. The National Telephone Company had an exchange in North Street and the Portsmouth Corporation had one in Brockhampton Lane. Calls between the two and all trunk calls were made through the post office exchange in Portsmouth. By 1915 the two companies had been taken over by the post office and a new exchange was installed at their premises in West Street. It does not appear to have been an instant success as a 1917 minute of the Havant Tradesmen's Association records that consideration was being given to recommending their members to disconnect because of its 'uselessness from a business point of view'.

Banks started to appear in the town in the 18th century but they were usually small companies that either collapsed or were taken over by others. The Hampshire Banking Company, which opened a branch at No.4 West Street in 1863, became the Capital and Counties Bank in 1878 and was taken over by Lloyds Bank in 1918. The present building dates from 1883. Barclays Bank arrived in 1907 and moved to its present building in East Street in 1911. The National Provincial Bank built, in the 1920s, the imposing premises at the corner of North and West Streets now occupied by the National Westminster Bank.

Having a local coastline was an added natural asset for Havant. Fish and shellfish provided a varied food supply and Langstone developed as a port for the town. Boats carried corn, wool and leather products to the rest of the country, bringing back wine, coal and building materials.

In addition to fishing, the recovery and sale of shingle was an important business which continued until the late 1930s. Barges sailed from Langstone to be grounded on the shingle banks where they were loaded by hand. Returning on the rising tide, the shingle was unloaded onto the quay with the aid of wheelbarrows. The remains of one barge *The Langstone* can still be seen, near to the old windmill, gently rotting away in the mud.

Also here was the crossing point to Hayling Island which, inhabited since pre-Roman times, was probably once joined to the mainland. As it became an island, access was increasingly difficult so a wadeway was built, possibly in the early Roman period. Constructed of flint and chalk with its route marked by oak posts, it can still be seen running from near the bottom end of Langstone High Street. The still visible gap in the middle, which was cut after the authorisation of the Portsmouth to Arundel section of the Portsmouth to London canal in 1817, made passing difficult except at low water and therefore placed more reliance on the ferry boat.

The canal company was supposed to have built a bridge to Hayling but, as they had not done so, they were made to contribute towards the wooden trestle toll bridge which was built by the Hayling Bridge Company and opened in 1824. This bridge, which had been taken over by the L.B.S.C.R. in 1878, was replaced by the present one in 1956 but the toll charges, still the same as in 1824, stayed until 1960. The Portsmouth to London canal was not a success and operated for less than ten years.

Havant's first hospital was an isolation hospital which was built at the end of Potash Terrace next to the railway line. It opened in 1894 and became known locally as the 'fever hospital'. Following its closure in 1939 the site and buildings were taken over by the Council and used as their works depot.

At the outbreak of the First World War an auxiliary military hospital was established at Langstone Towers, Langstone High Street, which continued in service until 1919. After the war there was considerable agitation in the town for a hospital to be built as a memorial to the local men who had lost their lives in the conflict. Many fundraising events were organised but it was not until 1927 that sufficient money was available for a start to be made. The site in Crossway was obtained and the Havant War Memorial hospital opened in 1929. A particularly fine feature of the children's ward, which was added in 1935, is a frieze of nursery rhymes depicted on Wedgwood tiles.

Associated with medical care was a number of friendly societies who, in return for a weekly subscription, gave financial support in time of sickness or paid hospital and doctors' fees. Many public houses ran 'slate clubs' whose yearly highlight was the Annual General Meeting when the landlord would lay on refreshments and the unused money from the previous year would be shared out among the members. However, the rules were very strict and onerous; you were not allowed to go out after dark or leave town without permission, otherwise your benefit would be stopped.

The Recreation Ground was opened in 1889 after the Local Board of Health purchased and had laid out four separate pieces of land, and traders donated the pavilion which opened the following year. Havant Cricket Club was formed in 1876, first playing on Sir Frederick Fitzwygram's private wicket at Leigh Park before moving to the Recreation Ground. Havant Football Club was probably formed around this time and was the forerunner of the Havant Eclipse, Havant Rovers, Havant United and Havant Town football clubs. St Faith's church ran football and cricket clubs under the name of Havant Red Star, and shop assistants taking advantage of their weekly half-day off made up the Havant Wednesday football and cricket clubs.

Havant Rovers football club usually played in the Recreation Ground but for a short time in the 1920s they moved to one of Farmer Russell's meadows in New Lane. Needing to give their venue a name they christened it Oak Park, the name by which it is still known today, after all the oak trees. The Rovers also had a cricket team but they had to play on Stockheath Common because the Recreation Ground was considered to be the sole preserve of the Havant Cricket Club. However permission was later given for them to play on alternate Sundays.

Havant Hockey Club was formed in 1905 and Havant Rugby Football Club in 1951. Clubs for cycling, athletics, bowls, tennis, shooting and many other activities have been formed over the years and many individuals and teams have achieved national and international success.

Between 1939 and 1945 Havant played its full part in the war effort. Thousands of service personnel were billeted in purpose-built camps or private houses. A searchlight station and anti-aircraft batteries were set up and for a time there was a Bofors gun in the middle of the roundabout by the present Civic offices. A first-aid post was established in St Faith's church hall, a British restaurant (Government café) was opened in the Nissen huts in Park Way, which is now a DIY store, and air raid shelters were erected in the Recreation Ground.

The Lavant stream, which had been so important in peacetime, was dammed 'for the duration of the hostilities' to provide a 'static water supply' for firefighting. The S.W.S. sign can just be seen on the wall at the junction of Elm Lane and Park Road North. Many tanks passed through the town and some left their mark by chipping the kerbstones on the south side of East Street and gouging the wall in the East Pallant.

The railway goods yard worked hard to cope with the large influx of material for D-Day and afterwards witnessed the sad sight of 'displaced persons' from Estonia, Latvia and Lithuania lining up to walk to their camp at Bedhampton and an uncertain future.

It has not been possible to record all of Havant's rich history in such a short space but it is hoped that this brief recital and the pictures that follow will inspire the reader to explore further.

1. The oldest building in Havant town is the 12th-century church of St Faith. Renovations during the 19th century exposed evidence of an earlier Roman structure, thus giving credence to the belief that the ancient crossroads were, in times past, the centre of a small Roman community. This picture dates from around 1910.

2. An interior view of the church shows, at its far end, the 13th-century chancel which is the oldest remaining section of the building. Havant traditionally celebrated the feast day of St Faith, 6 October, with an annual fair which was held in what is now Fairfield Road. The last fair was held in 1871.

3. On 7 June 1906, Canon Samuel Scott officiated at the wedding of his daughter Ellen to the Rev. Bernard Keymir. The large, predominantly female crowd, is hoping for a glimpse of the newlyweds as they leave St Faith's. Samuel Scott was Rector of St Faith's from 1892 until his retirement in 1915.

4. The reason for this gathering is obscure, although it would appear to be an 'after church' social occasion when pleasantries could be exchanged and 'Sunday best' clothing worn and admired. The location is, of course, the Havant crossroads with St Faith's church just out of view to the left of the picture.

5.   Sited in South Street is *The Old House At Home*. Although the date of 1339, displayed on its walls, is too early by about 200 years, the building is nevertheless reputed to be the oldest domestic building in Havant. Around 1900 there was a doss house at the rear where men could stay for 4d. a night. At the outbreak of war, in 1914, a travelling German oompah band left their dancing bear with the landlord before returning home!

6. The jettied upper storey of *The Old House At Home* was originally thatched but is otherwise little altered externally. In the early 1960s, petrol storage tanks, once used by the garage seen on the left, were discovered beneath the floorboards causing much consternation amongst local safety officers.

7. The ladies in the photograph are seen passing the *Speed the Plough*. Yet another public house, the *Anchor*, can also be noted almost opposite *The Old House At Home*.

8. A final view of South Street at its lower end with St Faith's in the background. Following the construction of the Havant by-pass in 1965, the street became a cul-de-sac, so sealing off this ancient route which once linked Havant with Hayling Island via its pre-historic wadeway.

9. Havant Rectory was later used as premises for St Nicholas's private school. Following the closure and demolition of the school, the site has been developed as Juniper Square, a pleasant modern development adjacent to South Street.

10. A mid-1930s aerial view shows Havant Rectory with its substantial walled garden. Grove Road can be seen running left to right towards the top of the picture with Orchard Road bisecting it.

11. The Central Stores on the left-hand corner of North Street is one of three differing properties to have occupied the site; since 1900 the most recent being that of the National Westminster Bank. At its rear, two terraced houses have been replaced with shops while, opposite, the Church Institute has been converted into business premises. *The White Hart* appears on the right-hand corner.

12.   Moving a little further into North Street, the long redundant *George Inn* can be seen on the left, its name still emblazoned in the upper masonry. The two dark painted shops facing the old *George Inn* are also still evident and trade today as a dress shop and jewellers.

13.   This 1920s view of North Street shows, on the left, the bay-windowed house and office of the local registrar, Mr. Best, who was succeeded by his daughter, Madge Best. The sun-blind opposite belongs to the premises of Vine's the butcher which vied with the pork butcher Standing, located next door.

14. The 'top' (north) end of North Street is little changed from this photograph, although the Foden steam brewers' dray belonging to Gale's no longer delivers to the *Star Inn*. The distant railway crossing gates were removed when the station was reconstructed and modernised in 1938. Prince George Street can be seen to the right.

North Street & Congregational Church, Havant.

15. Looking south from the last location, almost all of the west (right hand) side of North Street has been redeveloped. Built in 1890, the Congregational (now United Reform) church still stands together with its immediate neighbours, the two shop premises. The Empire Cinema is the light-coloured building past Glynn Martin, the estate agent adjacent to the church.

16. To obtain this view, which is directed towards Havant's eastern boundaries, the photographer stood on the railway bridge in East Street. In 1993 the bridge remains, although the Havant to Hayling railway line which once passed beneath closed in November 1963.

17. On a site previously occupied by East End House, the present Havant post office was opened in 1936. The premises were enlarged in the post-war years to cater for the needs of an expanding community.

18. A rare and unusual feature of the post office building is the Royal Cypher of His Majesty King Edward the Eighth above the original entrance. It remains a unique and constant reminder of a king who was never crowned. There is only one other Edward the Eighth post office in the country.

19. Alfred Wade, pictured *c.*1890 at premises which fronted his carriage hire business at No.23 South Street, who should not be confused with Mr. Wood, Havant's posting master in nearby East Street. Mr. Wade acted as posting master for mail which was passed between Havant and Hayling Island. A family connection is still maintained at this same location where a descendant now operates a motor repair business the workshops and yard which had previously housed horses and carriages.

20. A short distance from the apparent tranquility displayed in Plate 22, East Street shows its other face; that of a busy commercial district bordering on the town's centre.

21. This card postmarked 1913 shows an increase in the hoardings and advertisements on the sides of these East Street shops, the most evident being Veare the bootmaker.

22. Pictured in 1912, the traditionally quiet, residential end of East Street displays a variety of building styles including properties which have Victorian, Georgian, and even earlier origins of timber-framed construction.

23. One of the businesses trading in East Street in the early years of this century was Whittington's Bakery. There was also another branch in West Street.

24. William Pink, who had many shops in the Portsmouth area, took over Collins' Italian Warehouse in East Street in the 1920s. The premises along with Whittington's Bakery which was to the left were demolished in the 1930s and replaced with the single-storey building which stands today.

25. The *Bear Hotel*, an early coaching inn and posting house, still trades in East Street today. This postcard of *c*.1912 shows taxis belonging to the hotel awaiting fares. Mr. Dubois was the proprietor of the hotel as well as the Dubois wine shop.

26. West Street was and
still is the longest
thoroughfare in the town.
This and the following
pictures show it to have been
the principal shopping
district and it still remains so
today. A lady is seen on the
clean, frequently swept
cobbled crossing which
pedestrians were
encouraged to use rather
than the often muddy
roadway.

27. A suggested date for this
view is 1911 when the streets
were bedecked with national
flags for the coronation of
King George V. Citizens of
Havant needed little excuse
for a display of bunting.
Each and every civic
occasion would seem to
demanded evidence of their
loyalty.

28. West Street now lacks the premises of Pullen & Rose, Millers and Corn Merchants, which were sited immediately alongside St Faith's graveyard and can be seen on the left of the picture. The location can now be identified through the wide pavement and improved access to the Homewell.

29. Continuing in a westerly direction, the photographer is approaching the present junction of West Street with Park Road. In addition to the *Hearts of Oak*, a second hostelry, *The Fountain*, was located almost opposite at this time. Herington's, the haberdashery store, is included on the left.

30. Whilst the absence of motor vehicles is evident, an indication that the age of the car was imminent is the advertisement for 'Best American Petroleum Oil' displayed on the timber-faced building which still exists. At this time petroleum spirit would be stored and sold from two-gallon cans; the dispensing pump as yet unapproved. The man on the left is William Fay.

WILLIAM FAY,
Plumber and Decorator.

LEAD, GLASS, OIL, & COLOUR STORES

Art Wall Paperhangings & Decorations.
GLASS CUT TO ANY SIZE.

Paints Prepared Ready for Use.

West Street, HAVANT

31. An advertisement which appeared in the local trade directory.

32. This turn of the century postcard shows West Street viewed in an easterly direction. Opposite the previously mentioned *Hearts of Oak*, the *Fountain Inn* sign can be seen.

33. Much of the left-hand side of the road, including the *Dolphin Hotel* which was demolished in 1958, has been developed and re-developed to create the new Meridian Shopping Centre. The buildings opposite still remain, albeit in a different guise.

34. The large white house was the home and surgery of Dr. Norman and other doctors until the 1950s. A modern block of shops now stands on the site alongside the pedestrian access to the multi-storey car park.

35. When Dr. Norman lay ill in his West Street home, c.1915, straw was laid on the road outside to deaden the noise of iron-wheeled carts passing by. This picture, taken opposite his home, is no doubt of the straw arriving.

36.   A view of the *Dolphin Hotel* taken *c*.1918. Long's the butchers, located opposite the hotel, displayed their meat outside, in comparison to the rival London Central Meat Market with their window advertisement for Canterbury lamb.

37.   Dominating West Street in 1919 were the premises of the Post Office, built in 1892, and the Capital & Counties Bank, built in 1883. The telephone exchange was installed in the post office in 1915. The lower frontages of both properties have since been modernised in keeping with current trends and whilst banking is still carried on in the original premises, the post office is now a 'High Street' multiple electrical retailer.

38.   Returning through West Street, this picture was taken outside *The Black Dog* in the early 1900s. Local magistrates met at this public house where the Petty Sessional Courts were held. Civic meetings also took place here prior to the building of the Town Hall in 1870. Interior alterations in 1972 revealed an impressive Tudor doorway and timber framing which still remain today. The Wesleyan church appears opposite.

39.   Moving further from the town centre, West Street now reveals a residential character which continues until the termination of the street at the railway crossing. The white building was the Union Workhouse, first documented in 1811, which closed in 1936. Its next door neighbour is the police station. The unusual red (rather than blue) lamp is now re-located in the social club at the new police station.

40.   Examples of early council housing, nicknamed 'the white city', are seen in this 1926 photograph of West Street, which appears to have a road surface not yet treated with a macadam dressing.

41. H. J. Cooper, a local harness maker and saddler, carried on his business from these premises in North Street. Competition in the form of George Woolgar, harness maker and saddler, existed in nearby West Street.

42. Possibly less expensive to run and maintain than the horse-drawn cart, J. Loader of West Street chose to use a hand-propelled box cart. Oven space, at the baker's, was made available at Christmas time when Mr. Loader's customers could have their poultry cooked for 6d. per bird. This postcard dates from *c.*1910.

43. Less familiar now is the sight of door-to-door bread deliveries. Increasing awareness of the need for hygiene has rendered this traditional method both antiquated and unprofitable for the giant multiples which presently dominate the market. Archibald Parsons is the delivery man in this photograph.

44. The premises of Preston Watson & Co. in North Street, photographed in 1916. Mr. Preston Watson is seen sporting a lengthy beard.

45. The interior of Preston Watson.

46. Delivery wagon and crew pictured outside the Preston Watson wine shop, 1916.

47. Mr. and Mrs. Watson are seen posing with members of the Shoesmith family whilst motoring in Fairfield Road, c.1916. Jack Shoesmith is seated at the wheel.

48. Biden & Co., one of the larger local breweries, making a delivery to *The Yew Tree Inn* in Stoke Village, Hayling Island.

49. Sent Christmas 1910, this postcard is a fine study of St Joseph's Roman Catholic church and members of its clergy.

50. St Joseph's Roman Catholic church, presbytery and school was established in West Street, 1875.

51. West Street terminates at the railway crossing which forms a natural division between Havant and Bedhampton. Methodists have long since abandoned their chapel, where the last service was held in 1958, which still stands although severely vandalised. The signalman's hut was eventually removed in 1979 following the installation of automatic barriers in 1974.

52. 1936 is given as an approximate date for this picture. It will be seen that St Faith's church occupies the same relative position in the town as does the cathedral in Chichester, with West Street running parallel to the church. Both buildings are located on sites which have an earlier Roman influence.

53. This aerial view of North Street, taken in the 1920s, shows the level crossing at the top, and the Star Meadow just south of the railway on the left with marquees for some event. The market on the right was abolished during redevelopment.

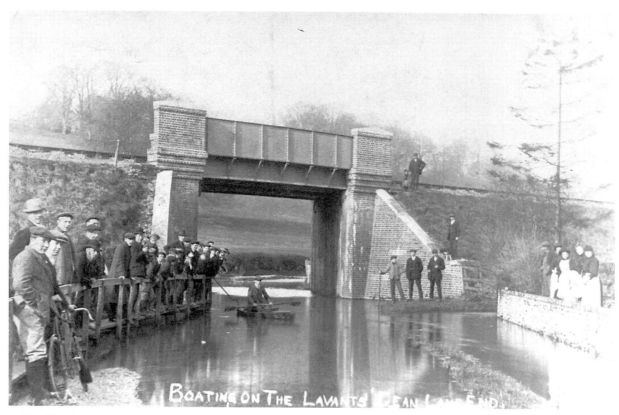

54. Flooding at Dean Lane End in 1912 caused by the periodic natural phenomenon of the Lavant Springs rising above their normal levels.

55. During unusually wet seasons the chalk of the Southern Downlands fails to absorb all of the rain which would normally percolate through to the lower levels, resulting in extensive flooding of the local streams, countryside and roads.

56. The permanent dry walkways constructed in Woodbury Lane, Rowlands Castle prove that flooding was a regular occurrence as shown by this 1912 picture.

57. The swollen Lavant stream continued its journey to the coast using an open ditch in North Street as its principle route. One can discern the duckboard walkways on the right of this picture which was taken before the Congregational church was constructed in 1890. It is recorded that on 27 November 1852 the flood was exceptionally high and a boat plied in North Street for two days.

58. Despite a plan of 1879 to divert the course of the stream, flooding continued to cause distress to householders. Water can be seen actually flowing through these houses in West Street when flooding was caused when a raft of planks and barrels, made by local youths, became lodged beneath Starr Bridge.

59. Scenes such as these in West Street, 1914, showing the flooded premises of J. Loader the baker, are unlikely to be repeated. Water is now commercially extracted from the countryside. Deep boreholes, providing for increased domestic and industrial use, have resulted in a general lowering of the natural water table.

60. Local leisure and sporting activities were given a valuable boost in 1888 when the Havant Local Board purchased several acres of meadowland for use as a recreation ground. The resulting Havant Park has continued to be a cherished amenity for more than 100 years.

61. Enjoying a cricket match in Havant Park before the outbreak of the First World War.

62.   The sports committee, formed to organise the many events which took place, are pictured here in 1912 each with rosette and buttonhole flowers. Their president, the popular Canon Samuel Scott, Rector of Havant, is seated left of centre.

63.   The judging panel are possibly awarding points at a cycle race during Havant Sports in 1912, whilst a competitor appears to be *hors-de-combat* with a foot problem.

64. A popular event enjoyed particularly by the spectators was the 'pillow fight', which was fought with heavily-filled sacks. The signal gantry to the right of the picture indicates the close proximity to the railway.

65. In an age when entertainment was provided by the people, for the people, Havant Sports Day was the most important occurrence in the social calendar. This scene dates from 1912.

66. Havant Sports in 1913. The ladies' hats are not quite as elaborate as those in the previous picture. Nevertheless, all these spectators are attired in their best clothes for the occasion.

67. Wealthy families and their guests could view the sports from a superior vantage point provided by the motor cars. In this 1914 view, the onlookers seem oblivious of the horrors to come with the outbreak of war.

68.   Members of the crowd who stayed to witness the prizegiving include the official photographer (left), who is almost certainly a journalist, to judge by the uniform trilby and raincoat worn by the members of the press. It is interesting to note that no one is seen without a hat.

REFRESHMENTS
H. HOLT, Caterer.
DOLPHIN HOTEL.

69.   Competitors at another sports day are applauded as they descend the pavilion steps with their trophies; the customary toast-rack for the gentleman and probably a boxed set of teaspoons for the lady.

70.   Cycling was a popular sport before the introduction of pneumatic tyres and there are references to a Havant Bicycle Club in the 1870s. This photograph was taken *c*.1912 in front of the *Brown Jug*, East Street. The motorcyclist is probably the pace-maker and speed recorder.

GEO CALE & CO LTD.   ALES & STOUT

71. This postcard is not of the Avenue Tennis Club, Warblington, now the principle club in the Havant district, but is the present day general store in Fourth Avenue. This store was part of the proposed leisure complex described on the postcard below.

72. This advertisement appeared on the reverse of the previous postcard, *c.*1910. Its glowing references to the proposed amenities seem to have gathered little support as the proprietor's ambitions were never fully realised.

POST CARD

To Motorists especially.

The DENVILLE SPORTS AND SOCIAL CLUB (Registered) to develop the following Sports, etc.;

Motoring :-Garage ; Lock-ups ; Repairs and Replacements supply, etc.

TENNIS : Covered, Hard and Grass Courts. Bowling Greens ; Badminton, from **4** to **8** Courts. Roller Skating. Racquets Courts.

CLUB : **25** Bedrooms, Bath Rooms, Reception Rooms, Club-room for Dancing, Concerts, Whist Drives, etc. ; Refreshment Bars ; Tea Lounge, etc. Billiards.

The Club can also Co-Operate Stores of Groceries, Provisions, Butchers, Greengrocery, Tobaccos, Library, Newsagent, Corn, Hardware, Clothing, etc.

Why not enjoy life on your own profits? Watch Advertisements in "Evening News."

Enquiries to--R. H. STAGG, Proprietor.
'Phone : HAVANT **85**.

73.   The Havant Eclipse football team was formed from the Havant Football Club and is reputed to have been the first winner of the Portsmouth Senior League in 1900. They were later absorbed into Havant Rovers football club.

74. Members of the Havant Eclipse football team in the 1903-4 season. The player with the Portsmouth club badge in the back row, last on the right, was probably a guest player.

Havant Rovers Football Club.

Ground: HAVANT PARK.

'Phone: Havant 514.

"HILLSBORO,"
23 LOWER GROVE ROAD,
HAVANT.

DEAR SIR,

You have been selected to play at *St. Faith's Meadow*

Saturday *25·2·39* Versus *Vospers* *South St.*

Kick-off *3 P.M.* Meet at *Ground* *Havant*

Kindly communicate at once if unable to play.

W. T. RUTTER, *Hon. Sec.*

75. An invitation to play for the Havant Rovers football club signed by their long-serving secretary, Billy Rutter.

76.   The opening in 1890 of the Recreation Ground Pavilion, which had been subscribed for by Havant tradesmen, was celebrated with a cricket match between Havant Local Board councillors and Portsmouth Town councillors. Havant scored 86 runs against Portsmouth's forty-three. The Portsea Island Union Workhouse Band provided musical entertainment. The president of Havant cricket club, Dr. J. Norman, is the last man on the right in the back row, and Sir Frederick Fitzwygram is leaning against the post in the pavilion.

77.   Founder members of the Bellair bowling club, 1908. Pictured among the group is young Gus Cousins, whose duties at the club included marking at billiards for which he apparently received 1d. per hour.

78. Havant cricket club in the 1929-30 season.

79. Havant hockey team, 1930s.

80. The Old Town Mill, also known as Pullen's Mill, was a dominant feature of the landscape. It ceased milling in 1934 and was finally demolished in 1958.

81. The mill wheel was driven by a reserve of water contained in the millpond which in turn was fed by the Lavant Stream and two prolific local springs. The volume of water to the mill could be guaranteed and was often used to irrigate the lower meadows.

82. Abundant supplies of clear fresh water created employment in a variety of ways. The growing and marketing of healthy watercress for Covent Garden, Hampshire and Sussex markets gave this small industry a reputation which survived for many years. Mr. Harry Marshall is seen gathering his harvest.

83. This pathway alongside the watercress beds in the Lymbourne stream was a favourite route to the sea shore.

84. Fresh water from the chalk downs together with the skins of sheep which once grazed these downs presented Havant with the ingredients necessary for producing parchment. It is recorded that the Treaty of Versailles was signed on Havant parchment which was reputed to be the best quality in the world. The remarkable whiteness of the parchment has been attributed to the chalk content of water used from Homewell spring. These three photographs date from 1926.

85. Probably produced here since Roman times, the method changed very little. Soaked in a lime and water solution of increasing strength, the skins were treated in this way for three weeks.

86. At the end of this period, the skins were scraped with knives to remove surplus fat, then stretched upon frames 6ft. by 4ft. to dry before continuing the lengthy curing process.

87. Employees of Messrs. Stallard, Parchment Manufacturers are seen grouped for this company photograph, *c*.1910. Stallard remained in business until 1936.

88. *(above right)* This picture shows local lasses who worked at Stent's Glove Factory in the 1930s. From left to right; Laurie Green, Queenie Pink, Bete Sawyer, Eileen Simmons, Vi Stevens, Dos Banbury, Matty Wellman, Dora Roper, Grace Roper, Kate Banbury.

89. A cast photograph of a local stage production by Havant Dramatic Society.

90. A delightful scene showing the local May Queen and her attendants photographed by George Pratt, *c.*1930.

91. The Havant Fanciers Society staged an annual show in the Town Hall. This photograph of the 1912 event, however, is not thought to have been taken in that building.

92. James Newell, greengrocer of West Street, was the owner of this stagecoach which contributed to the fun at fundraising parades in the 1930s.

93. The earliest form of public cinema was the bioscope. Located briefly in the Star Meadow, Walter Payne's Dreamland offered escape into the celluloid world of adventure with epics such as *The Female Spy*, *Policeman's Run* and *The Witches Cave*. A bioscope such as this can still be visited each summer season at Hollycombe near Liphook, Hants.

94. In 1893 an Isolation (fever) hospital was built adjacent to Potash Terrace. As it was restricted to patients with contagious and infectious diseases, sufferers in need of medical and surgical treatment would have to travel to Emsworth or Portsmouth hospitals.

95. World War One saw the establishment of an Auxiliary Military hospital when Langstone Towers was loaned to the nation by the Stent family. During the four years of its existence almost 1,500 sick and injured servicemen received treatment here. Were this a colour photograph, the patients would be seen wearing the bright blue uniform issued to hospitalised service personnel.

96. Following the war it was decided that a Memorial hospital should be built at Havant as a practical and permanent reminder of those who had sacrificed their lives. The town's oldest citizen, centenarian Miss Sarah Bannister, was chosen to turn the first sod on 16 November 1927.

97. On 27 July 1929 Sarah Bannister attended the dedication of the completed building. Fund raising had continued in the town from 1919 and it can be truthfully said that the hospital was funded entirely by public subscription.

98. One of the many fund-raising events for the Memorial hospital was a comic football match involving local sportsmen who donned this astonishing variety of fancy dress for the occasion. Team changes displayed are, Viper Allen (Out of work Nomads) substitute for Willie Stevens. Ginger Reeves (Firewood Reserves) substitute for Daisy Smith!

99. Another charity football match to raise funds for the Memorial hospital in the early 1930s.

100. A Boxing Day comic cricket match at the recreation ground was played in the style of The Hambledon Club. The event was staged in support of the Memorial hospital.

101. This engraving depicts the original
Leigh Park House, *c*.1860.

102. The magnificent Gothic library
remained *in situ* following the demolition of
the house. Serious attempts are now being
made to restore this fine building after years
of neglect and vandalism.

103.   A second Leigh Park House was constructed in 1863 on a site north of the original location. Of striking appearance and mammoth proportions, the mansion failed to reach its centenary, being declared 'too costly to maintain' by the owners, Portsmouth City Council. The demolition in 1959 has since been considered an error of judgement and an act of folly.

104.   The Sir George Staunton country park has now been created whereby the landscaped gardens and decorative lake of the Leigh Park Estate can be enjoyed by today's and future generations.

105. When mains drainage was installed in West Street and traffic temporarily diverted through Havant Park, *c*.1910, the ornamental fountain seen here was removed to the home of a local councillor for safe keeping. It was never returned to the park.

106. During the period in which the fountain graced the garden of this Bedhampton residence, it became a feature enjoyed by Stirling Stent, his family and friends. Massive in construction, it would seem difficult to lose but nevertheless it has disappeared, leaving no clue to its ultimate fate or destination.

107. The water source which powered Havant Town Mill, continuing toward the Langstone shore, also drove the wheel of West Mill seen in this picture. Originally the site of an earlier fulling mill which was destroyed by fire, this picture is of a flour mill; built in 1823, it was demolished in 1936.

108. Langstone High Street gives access to the shore and the ancient wadeway which leads to Hayling Island. It also enables visitors to seek the old watermill and windmill which are adjacent to *The Royal Oak Inn*.

109.   Unloading shingle at Langstone harbour.

110.   The inn, whilst enjoying a favoured position on the shoreline, is sometimes forced to suffer the floods brought about by storms and exceptionally high tides.

111. Well known to generations of
painters and photographers, the windmill
is unusual in that its neighbour was a
watermill fed by the Lymbourne stream
and millpond.

112. Abandoned and neglected since at
least the mid-19th century, the mill
remained a picturesque ruin, complete
with resident ghost.

113. Happily, Langstone mill was saved from further deterioration when it was purchased in 1932 by Flora Twort, a well-known Petersfield artist, who spent years of dedication in rebuilding and converting the old premises into living accommodation and studio. Flora, seen in this self portrait, entertained many famous personalities including Neville Shute, who wrote *The Pied Piper* during his lengthy war-time stay at the mill.

114. Pictured from the toll bridge, the shore at Langstone is a panorama which includes the *Ship Inn*, *The Royal Oak Inn* and the Old Windmill.

115. Shingle dug by hand from the local Winner Bank was taken to Langstone. Here carts are waiting to be loaded.

116. The road bridge linking Hayling Island with Havant was opened in 1824, a toll being imposed on all vehicles approaching from the mainland. This picture dates from *c.*1915.

117.   A lorry delivering cans of petroleum spirit to Hayling is paying its toll at the bridge barrier gate. The payment of tolls finally ceased on 11 April 1960.

118.   The railway swing bridge which connected Hayling Island with the mainland. Manually operated, it is shown open for the passage of a sailing boat, c.1932.

119.   With the foundation of the Havant and Waterloo Urban District, the Ford Balco engine (the first motor fire-engine) became based at Waterlooville and a replacement engine, a Merryweather Albion was supplied to Havant at a cost of almost a thousand pounds. This picture was taken outside the station at Park Road North.

120. Gordon Till road-testing the second Havant fire-engine in 1932.

121. The coronation of King George V prompted this parade on 22 June 1911. The marchers in North Street include a contingent drawn from the local public services with representative firemen, postmen and railway employees.

122. One of many fund-raising efforts. In this shot, *c.*1915, of West Street all forces unite; friendly societies, Oddfellows, firemen, railwaymen and postmen to collect money for Portsmouth and Emsworth hospitals.

123.   Friendly societies in West Street. The building on the left was a registry office for servants.

124.   The procession is seen passing the Union Workhouse in West Street.

125. Coming to rest in the recreation ground, the banner is displayed by supporters and members of the Independent Order of Oddfellows, Manchester Unity. An appeal notice for the hospital fund can be noted on the right.

126.   A military band and marching men generate support and admiration from the onlookers on the corner by St Faith's church.

127.   A bicycle detachment of the 9th Hampshire Regiment is pictured near the railway station en route to camp in 1913.

128.   The local street sweepers will be kept busy following this visiting parade of cavalry passing through North Street.

129. Military personnel were again present on 30 September 1922 when the town's war memorial was dedicated to the memory of local men who gave their lives. Havant lost 101 men in the First World War and 50 in the Second World War.

130. The memorial was unveiled by Major General Sir John Davidson K.C.M.G., D.S.O., M.P. at a service conducted by the Rector of Havant, Rev. H. N. Rodgers during which the memorial was committed to the care of the local authority.

131. Older readers will recall the eagerness with which Empire Day, held on 24 May, Queen Victoria's birthday, was welcomed each year. The occasion was celebrated nationwide with parades and demonstrations of loyalty staged by the military, school children and employees of public utilities. Part of the 1927 celebrations held in Havant recreation ground are captured in this picture.

132. St Faith's Drum and Fife Band, 1896. The bandmaster is Mr. Hann.

133. The Scouting movement was founded in 1908 to develop character, practical skills and self reliance in young men. The 1st Havant troop sponsored by St Faith's church was formed in 1919 and led by Admiral Nugent.

134. George Chaffer pictured here in 1950 when over 80 years old. A familiar Sunday morning figure, he is seen delivering Sunday newspapers in Waterloo Road. The old Hygeia Laundry forms part of the background.

135. John Parsons joined Hants. Police on 11 July 1880. He was promoted to the rank of sergeant in 1896 despite irregular conduct at West Cowes in 1882 (for which he was fined two days' pay) and being in a public house when he should have been on duty in 1883 (which cost him four days' pay). He was sergeant at Havant from 1902 until he left the force in 1906. His son was Archibald Parsons who delivered bread locally (*see* 39).

136.   Pupils and staff of Havant Church school in 1908.

137.   Pupils and staff of Havant Boys' school.

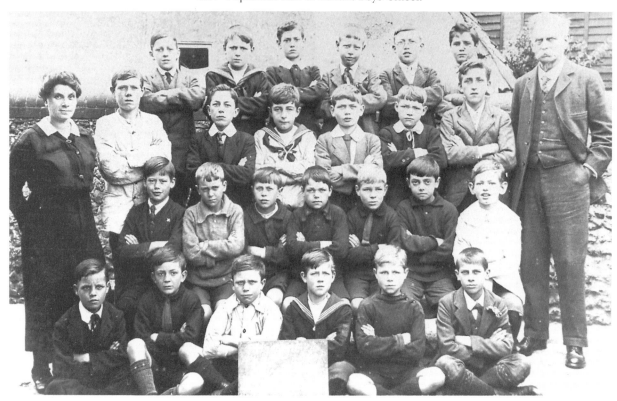

138. Headmaster of the Havant Council school, Harry Beeston, instilled into his pupils an appreciation and love of the countryside many years before our current trend for awareness of the environment. He is pictured with his 'Bird and Tree Gang' at one of their numerous tree-planting activities in 1908.

139. Miss Grace with her infants' class III, Havant National school in 1909.

140.   The entire Warblington school assemble for their annual photograph for the year 1906. The building still stands at the corner of Pook Lane and Emsworth Road and is used as a church hall.

141.   Members of the public, always on hand to witness the free entertainment to be found in local streets, watch navvies at work on drain digging in a heavily congested trench. The scene was recorded in The Pallant in 1907.

142. Following a hard day's work, these Havant 'worthies', possibly fortified by a visit to the *Six Bells*, found the courage to call at the studio of William Scorer. The resulting photograph is a fine character study of the period.

143.   Pipe laying for the drains, this time in North Street.

144.   Havant Council's Wallis and Steevens steamroller at work in the 1930s. The road mender with the broom is Bill New who claimed to have walked backwards down every road in Havant spraying hot tar from the tar boiler, prior to the granite chippings being laid and rolled.

145. Pictured in South Leigh Forest in 1899 are members of the Outen family who were well known and respected locally. Self employed, they are engaged in stripping felled timber of its bark which was always in demand in the local tanning industry. Baby Francis is concealed in the white bundle.

146. George and Mary Outen pose with 14 of their 15 children in the early 1920s. George also looked after the Cattle Market, made coffins for deceased workhouse inmates and assisted in taking them on a cart to the cemetery for burial.

147. The Outen family prepare to depart from Woodbine Cottage for one of their many weddings. The service was held at Warblington church, with the reception in a marquee erected in a field close to the family home.

148. Another well-known local family were the Cousins. Retail and wholesale newsagents, the Cousins supplied every Sunday newspaper sold in Havant between 1890 and 1988. Prior to 1950, the newspapers were to be bought only from the lounge of 84 West Street! Twelve out of their thirteen children are seen with Augustus and Edith Cousins. On weekdays, Augustus was a parchment worker.

149. Following the reclamation of the Mill Pond, Park Road South was opened for traffic in 1937. This less than busy junction has now undergone a complete change and is the principle route in and out of the town, carrying several thousand vehicles each day.

150. An important railway town since 1847, Havant provided station facilities and a goods yard for both the London Brighton South Coast and the London South Western Railways. The locomotives are pictured heading eastwards from the mainline platform and the goods yard in the early 1900s.

151. Buildings and platforms have been subjected to several changes. Here the station is seen prior to its 1938 rebuild. Hayling coaches are at rest at their own platform.

152. An early form of commuter service, Chichester to Portsmouth, came into being in 1906 when L.B.S.C.R. introduced the motor train. In addition to stations at Bosham and Emsworth, new halts were created at Fishbourne, Southbourne, Nutbourne and Bedhampton, followed in 1907 by Warblington.

153.   In principle the new motor train halts were a forerunner of our present-day bus stops, providing convenient access to rail services previously available only to users of mainline stations. This picture shows the motor train halt at Warblington.

154.   Prior to the 1938 re-vamp of Havant station, crossing gates were positioned at the 'top end' (north) of North Street. At the far side of the gates is Leigh Road leading to Rowlands Castle.

155.   This photograph of Havant station dates from 1888, the year before its first reconstruction. The station porter, Mr. S. Walder, later a guard on the Hayling line, is fourth from the right. The smallest of the three boys is an employee of W. H. Smith and worked from the station news stand.

156. Railway staff from Havant station who 'did their bit' by serving in the Forces in the First World War.

157. This most unusual vehicle, employed by L.B.S.C.R. as a rail inspection car, is operating on a section of line which, with rails and banks removed, is now the car park of Town End House in East Street.

158. From the early 1800s and onwards for over a hundred years, a blacksmith's forge was situated on this corner of South Leigh Road. With Warblington railway halt only a minute's walk away, railway posters and timetables were displayed on the wall of the smithy.

159. The Green Pond of the previous picture is seen again. This photograph also depicts the tiny Warblington school on the right.

160. With the added convenience of a railway halt at Warblington, the centuries-old 'Denfields' – the original name for the meadows north of the main road – were further developed to become the suburb of Denvilles. With the signal box just visible in the background, road improvements and the laying of mains services are underway to meet the expansion of this new community in this postcard of 1934.

161. Leigh Road, once a picturesque avenue of trees, provided a first view of the countryside for many Portsmouth folk who arrived by train at Havant to spend a day in the country. The sign indicates the road on the right to be West Leigh Road.

162. The magnificent avenue of trees which once graced the approach to Warblington Rectory has been ravaged by Dutch Elm Disease and sadly no longer contributes to the beauty of Hampshire's countryside.

163. Pook Lane, seen here *c.*1910, provided a route from the main Havant Road to the shore and one-time quay at Warblington. It is probable that a ferry once plied to and from Hayling Island as an alternative to the often perilous wadeway.

164. Often referred to as 'Spook Lane', Pook Lane and nearby Warblington Rectory both carry tales of mysterious hauntings. Whilst it has been suggested that the stories were circulated to deter local folk from frequenting both lane and shore where the smugglers' nocturnal activities took place, the Rectory can actually claim to have evidence of ghostly manifestations since 1695.

165. Now devoid of its trees, Church Lane (Warblington Lane), only seconds from the exceptionally busy South Coast Road, transports the visitor to the comparative peace and solitude surrounding the old castle, church and seashore.

166. A charming period study with Warblington's church of Thomas à Becket in the background, *c.*1910.

167. The church of St Thomas à Becket retains scant evidence of its early beginnings. An almost total 13th-century rebuild destroyed or concealed within its fabric much of the Saxon work which was not exposed again until a restoration in the 1830s.

168. The ancient wooden porch attracts many visitors and is reputed to date from c.1350.

169. Warblington Castle's most interesting owner was Margaret Pole, Countess of Salisbury, a cousin of Henry VIII. As a staunch Catholic, Margaret refused to condone Henry's marriage to Anne Boleyn, and was executed in 1543. It is reputed that she refused to kneel at the block. During the Civil War in 1643, Warblington Castle was severely 'slighted' by Parliamentary soldiers. All that survives now is one tower of the gatehouse.

170. One of the many wartime 'public awareness' events, the annual National Savings Week was intended to promote and encourage personal savings as an investment in the Nation's war effort. The 'driver' was Mr. Dick Smart who hand-built the steam engine. After the war Mr. Smart, known to many as 'grandad', used to give children rides along the Hayling Island seafront. The year of this picture, reproduced by courtesy of *The Portsmouth News*, is 1944 and the author, Ralph Cousins, is the small boy wearing the belted overcoat and school cap.

171.   The march-past which took place in Havant Park is believed to be part of a parade celebrating victory in Europe; the troops are possible members of the Home Guard Unit. (This photograph is reproduced by courtesy of *The Portsmouth News*.)

172.   Havant's pride suffered its greatest ever blow when it was announced that H.M.S. *Havant* had been sunk whilst evacuating troops from the Dunkirk beaches. Originally built for the Brazilian Navy, she was requisitioned by the Admiralty for service with the Royal Navy in 1939. Her short, though very active, career came to an end at 10.15 a.m. on 1 June 1940.

173. This fine aerial view of the new Market Parade development appeared in the *Hampshire Telegraph* on 27 June 1963.
Havant station is seen complete with goods yard and the Hayling Billy waits to depart from its own platform. To the
right of the station car park was the Star Meadow, venue for the travelling bioscope and funfairs. It was also the
location of the cattle market before it moved to the other side of North Street on the site of today's North Street Arcade.
(Reproduced with the permission of *The Portsmouth News*.)

Bibliography

Borough of Havant, *Town Trail Booklets* (Havant Borough Council, 1978-88)

Brown, A. M., *A Brief History of Havant* (published by author, 1946)

Dicken, Jill, *Chichester Harbour, The Thirteen Villages* (Chichester Harbour Conservancy, 1983)

Fairfield First School P.T.A., *Fairfield, Then & Now* (F.F.S. P.T.A., 1987)

Havant Local History Group, *The Making of Havant* (1987-92)

Joicey, Richard, *Harbour Sketches* (Ian Harrap, 1977)

Joicey, Richard, *Langstone, A Mill in a Million* (Ian Harrap, 1976)

Longcroft, Charles, *The Hundred of Bosmere* (1852)

Morley, John, *Old Langstone* (Langstone Village Association, 1983)

Morley, John, *Wadeway to Hayling* (Havant Borough Council, 1988)

Reger, A. J., *Havant & Bedhampton Past and Present* (Ian Harrap, 1975)

Reger, A. J., *The Liberty of Havant 1650-1852* (unpublished but available for research at Havant Museum)

Reger, A. J., *A Short History of Emsworth and Warblington* (1987)

Rogers, Peter, *Havant in Old Picture Postcards* (European Libraries, 1985)

Salter, Geoff and Dene, Derek, *Havant Seen & Remembered* (Hants County Libraries, 1979)

Salter, Geoff, *Leigh Park Gardens, The Sir George Staunton Estate* (Havant Borough Council, 1983)

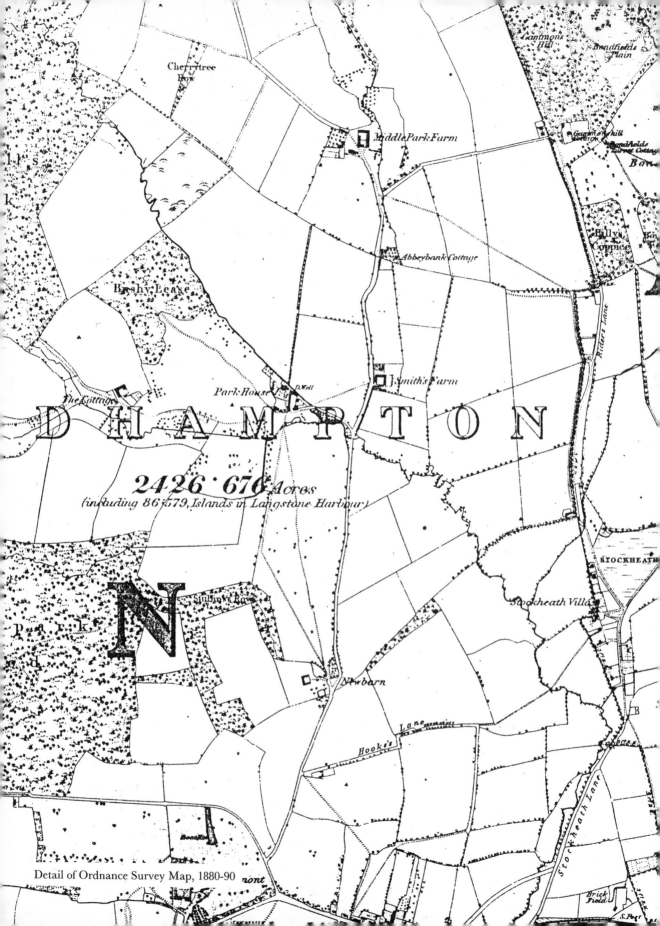

Detail of Ordnance Survey Map, 1880-90